Ming the Messenger

Illustrated by Justin Gerard

MW00514539

Target Skill Compare and Contrast

PEARSON

Scott Foresman

Ming is on the job!

He jumps on his bike.

Ming has work to do.

What is your first stop, Ming?

Good-bye!

Race on, Ming!

"What was that?" said Pam.

"What was that?" said Dad.

"It was Ming!" said Bob.

Ming zips past the park.

Ming zips past the batters.

Race on, Ming!

Ming is at his stop.

Look at his face!

"Hello, Ming!" said Ann.

Ann is glad to see Ming!

Ming hands Ann a small box.

Hop back on, Ming!

Where will Ming race to next?

Race home, Ming!